A PERSON OF NO CONSEQUENCE

A Play

by

MARGARET WOOD

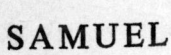

SAMUEL FRENCH

LONDON
NEW YORK   TORONTO   SYDNEY   HOLLYWOOD

ISBN 0 573 03369 2

MADE AND PRINTED IN GREAT BRITAIN BY
LATIMER TREND & COMPANY LTD PLYMOUTH

MADE IN ENGLAND

CHARACTERS

Mrs Hartley
Elizabeth, Mrs Hartley's pretty daughter
Elinor, Mrs Hartley's apparently plain and bespectacled
  niece
Lady Charlotte Wentworth
Mrs Browning
Mrs Nullis
Miss Jane
A Maid

NOTE: The prototypes of these characters (with the exception of Miss Jane herself) may be found in Miss Jane's novels. Mrs Browning has much of Mrs Bennet in her, and Lady Charlotte much of Lady Catherine de Burgh—both in *Pride and Prejudice*. Mrs Nullis resembles Mrs Norris of *Mansfield Park*, and Mrs Hartley is a composite character of several designing mothers. Elizabeth has something of Elizabeth Bennet in her, while Elinor owes much to Jane Austen's shyer, suffering heroines, such as Ann Elliott of *Persuasion* and Fanny Price of *Mansfield Park*

The action of the play takes place in the drawing-room of Mrs Hartley's house

Period—Regency

A PERSON OF NO CONSEQUENCE

The drawing-room of Mrs Hartley's house. The hour of the morning call

The furniture and furnishings are in Regency style. There is an elegant "Adam" fireplace in one wall, with a mirror above it, and a french window opposite. There is a door in the back wall. (See Set Plan and Furniture Plot on p. 21)

The CURTAIN *rises on a tableau, to sprightly music from a suitable composer (for instance, Haydn). This is held until the introductory music is finished—just long enough for the audience to realize that this* is *a tableau and to appreciate what should be an attractive Regency picture. Then the characters move into life*

Elizabeth is proferring a plate to Miss Jane, who is seated unobtrusively by the fireplace. Mrs Nullis is seated on the sofa, half turned to Mrs Hartley, who is behind the sofa, handing her a glass of madeira. Elinor sits forlornly over by the window. As the music fades, Mrs Nullis and Jane accept their refreshments with smiles and slight bows. Then the door is thrown open and the Maid announces

Maid Mrs Browning, ma'am.

Mrs Browning enters—a garrulous, rather silly woman, a-flutter with gossip. The Maid exits

Mrs Browning My dear Mrs Hartley, what a time I have had of it, to be sure. I thought I should never be here before the others had left, and then I should have missed all the news and had nothing to tell my dear husband over the luncheon table—not that he ever listens to a word I say, but then the girls love to hear of everything that goes on. Good morning to you, Mrs Nullis, and to you, Miss Jane. And Elizabeth.

Elizabeth bobs a curtsey

I vow, Mrs Hartley, your girl grows prettier every day. (*She sits*)

Mrs Hartley If she is half as pretty as your girls, Mrs Browning, I shall be satisfied.

Mrs Nullis Ah, there'll be some breaking of hearts where Miss Elizabeth is concerned, eh, Mrs Browning? Eh, Elizabeth?

Elizabeth (*turning away coldly to the table*) Indeed, ma'am, the only heart that is likely to be broken is my own.

Mrs Nullis (*avidly*) What's that? *Your* heart broken?

Mrs Browning La! What can the child mean?

Mrs Hartley (*sharply*) Elizabeth! You will not make these pert answers, especially to my guests.

Elizabeth It is not pertness, Mamma, but truth.

Mrs Browning (*wagging her finger at Elizabeth*) Ah. I see it all. I do not have pretty daughters of my own without learning a good deal. (*To Mrs Hartley*) The trouble is that they *will* develop minds of their own. I cannot think where they get them from.

Mrs Nullis (*sweetly*) From their father, perhaps. Certainly not from you, dear Mrs Browning.

Mrs Browning (*unaware of the shaft*) True. For he is perverse to a degree—for ever taking the girls' part against me, ridiculing any eligible young man I may find, or commending ones who are entirely impossible—merely to provoke me. I say to him, "Mr Browning," I say, "you have six daughters to dispose of, and how do you propose to provide for them if not by a good marriage?" And of course he has no reply, my dear, no reply at all. He just shakes out his newspaper and hides himself away.

Mrs Nullis But we were talking of Elizabeth. Why is your heart to be broken, my dear?

Elizabeth I am the last person to ask, Mrs Nullis, since I am forbidden to mention him at all.

Mrs Browning "Him." Aha.

Mrs Hartley Growing pains, growing pains, my dear Mrs Nullis. Hand some madeira to Mrs Browning, Elizabeth.

Elizabeth goes to the table and does so

We have a good match in hand for her—one that will set her up for life—and she will have none of it. A good establishment is nothing to her. A penniless naval lieutenant is her fancy, if you please.

Miss Jane A penniless lieutenant need not remain in that position, Mrs Hartley. I have two brothers in the Navy. Promotion is possible.

Mrs Hartley But not as rapid as that of the heir to a large estate whose father may be carried off by a fortunate apoplexy at any moment.

Elizabeth But I am not in love with him, Mamma.

Mrs Hartley Love? I am speaking of a permanent position in society, girl, not a momentary infatuation. Where would you be if your father and I had married for love?

Jane (*to herself*) A question to be pondered, indeed!

Elizabeth But I doubt that Mr Samson is in love with me, either. He may not wish to marry at all. That is *your* idea.

Mrs Nullis Nonsense, child. Any young man in possession of a large fortune must of course be in want of a wife.

Elizabeth Then, Mrs Nullis, let him look elsewhere. (*She moves to the window*)

Mrs Browning (*roguishly*) He will look long to discover a prettier one.

Mrs Nullis (*rising and moving to Elinor*) At least here is one who will give no trouble of that kind.

Elinor looks wretchedly up at Mrs Nullis through her spectacles

I always think how very just the good Lord is. To those to whom he cannot give good looks, he gives brains.

Elinor's lip trembles, and she looks down

Elizabeth (*turning on Mrs Nullis*) And to some, Mrs Nullis, he gives neither. (*She sits by Elinor's chair*)

Mrs Nullis (*offended*) Hoity toity! (*She moves back and sits*)

Mrs Hartley Elizabeth! Unless you can behave yourself with decorum you will go to your room. I will not have . . .

The door opens and the Maid, most impressed, enters

Maid Please, ma'am, Lady Charlotte Wentworth's carriage has just drawn up . . .

Mrs Hartley (*in awed delight*) Lady Charlotte!

Mrs Nullis and Mrs Browning rise excitedly

Lady Charlotte herself, my dears! To call! What an honour. I hardly expected . . . Excuse me, while I wait upon her.

Mrs Hartley hastens out after the Maid

Mrs Browning (*impressed*) Lady Charlotte! That is a feather in Mrs Hartley's cap. She seldom visits in the village.
Mrs Nullis Very seldom. She has never visited *me*!
Jane Lady Charlotte prefers to command attention in her own mansion.
Mrs Nullis But then she was born to command, was she not? Few of us are in that happy position.
Jane (*drily*) If it *is* happy. She does not strike me as a very happy woman.
Mrs Nullis Upon my word, madam, it is not for us to criticize our betters.
Jane (*quietly*) Betters . . . ?

Further argument is saved by the entrance of Lady Charlotte, attended by an obsequious Mrs Hartley

Mrs Hartley Friends! Lady Charlotte has done me the honour of calling. Lady Charlotte, may I introduce Mrs . . .

Mrs Nullis presses forward with an eager smile

Lady Charlotte Pray do not give yourself the trouble, Mrs Hartley. Some faces are familiar. Mrs Browning and her numerous daughters I have already met—and your daughter Elizabeth. The others I will enquire about as the need arises. (*Regarding the two girls through her lorgnettes*) Are these *both* your girls, Mrs Hartley?
Mrs Hartley Oh, no indeed. Only the pretty one—that is to say, Elizabeth, whom you have met.

Elizabeth bobs a curtsey, with no very good grace

The other is my niece, Elinor, my brother's child. He, poor man, was killed last year, when his horse bolted.

Elinor curtseys

Lady Charlotte Unfortunate. I disapprove of melodramatic deaths. They carry things to excess. (*She sits on the sofa*) So you have taken the burden of her upbringing upon you, Mrs Hartley?

They all sit again

Mrs Hartley (*piously*) It was no more than my duty. The person who will not succour another in distress . . .

Elizabeth (*rising angrily, but retaining Elinor's hand in hers*) It is no burden! Elinor is my dearest companion and a great help in the house. Since she came I——

Lady Charlotte (*interrupting*) I was speaking to your mother, miss. When I address you, you may address me. But not before. Mrs Browning, I trust *you* have taught your daughters when to be seen and not heard?

Elizabeth kneels and tries to comfort the humiliated Elinor

Mrs Browning To be sure I have, my lady. Though my husband *will* indulge them and take their part. I am sure I am forever telling them their manners and curbing their high spirits and trying to make them behave themselves like young ladies. But truth to tell, when you have beautiful daughters, and though I do not wish to boast mine are as comely as any in the district, it is no easy matter to keep them modest and retiring. For when the military are in town, my girls cannot walk down the street without a crowd of admirers following, and though I do not wish to boast——

Lady Charlotte (*interrupting*) Mrs Browning, you have twice said that you do not wish to boast, yet you continue to do so.

Mrs Browning subsides, at a loss

Mrs Hartley (*hurriedly*) Lady Charlotte, some madeira and a morsel of cake?

Lady Charlotte Thank you, I never eat or drink between meals. (*Rising and moving to the window*) You have a passably pretty little estate here, I notice. The approach is much improved.

Mrs Hartley (*delightedly joining her*) Ah yes, the improvements. We have made a sweepup to the house in a curve, instead of the old straight drive, which brought one to the door in no time at all. The new approach takes the horses almost twice as long to arrive at the entrance. It is altogether more impressive.

Lady Charlotte And there was some work going on at the opposite end of the garden. What might that be?

Mrs Hartley I am quite delighted that you noticed it, Lady Charlotte. We are creating a shrubbery there, with a ha-ha beyond it to avoid the necessity of a hedge or wall which would obscure the view of the little wilderness which we have contrived.

Lady Charlotte (*turning back into the room*) I would like to view these "improvements", as you call them, and give you the benefit of my considerable experience, as well as of my taste. I have carried out improvements on my own estate, though of course on a vast scale. However, no doubt I can reduce my ideas to the amount of space available . . .

Lady Charlotte and Mrs Hartley go

Mrs Browning and Mrs Nullis stare after them, then turn angrily to each other

Mrs Browning Well! Mrs Hartley appears to forget that she has other visitors, as soon as Lady Charlotte joins us.

Mrs Nullis Upon my soul, Mrs Browning, Lady Charlotte has quite forgot that she met me on the occasion of the dance at the Assembly Rooms, and again at Bath when we were there for the cure for my poor husband's gout, though to be sure it was no cure, for the gout went to his heart or his head or somewhere not six weeks after and carried him off, so all that expense was wasted. But Lady Charlotte was there, and that vulgar toadying woman Mrs Robinson introduced me to her ladyship. And now, if you please, she ignores me and goes off to look at a shrubbery instead. I'll not endure it. I am interested in shrubberies as much as the next person, I should hope. I shall join them.

Mrs Nullis goes out

Mrs Browning If she is joining them, I do not see why I should be left behind. (*To Jane*) Will you come, madam?

Jane Thank you, Mrs Browning, but my passion for shrubberies is limited. I shall find more to interest me here.

Mrs Browning Here? With no-one but the two girls? And they at the silliest age? You must jest, ma'am.

Mrs Browning goes out

Jane (*with a sigh, rising*) What *is* the silliest age in woman?

Elizabeth Evidently ours. You heard Mrs Browning.

Jane (*looking at the two girls*) I cannot agree with her. The silliest age of all is the woman of forty or so with daughters of a marriageable age; especially when she is hunting for an eligible son-in-law.

Elizabeth (*sighing*) That's Mamma.

Jane Equally silly are those who endure—nay actually desire—to be patronized by arrogant, selfish, bigoted old ladies.

Elizabeth Mamma again.

Jane Oh, do not mistake me, Elizabeth. I do not mean to criticize your mother in particular. You too will be much the same at her age. (*She sits on the sofa*)

Elinor Oh no, no.

Elizabeth Never!

Jane What other hope have you? I sometimes think that there is no place in the world where women are treated with so much contempt as in England.

Elinor Contempt? What can you mean?

Jane Why should not women be educated as their brothers are educated?

Elizabeth But men have to equip themselves to provide for their families. For a woman it is enough to read and write, is it not? Enough for a genteel woman with a family?

Jane (*rising, passionately*) No, it is *not*! A genteel woman will fill her pantry with good things and be content to leave her mind empty. And men are pleased enough that they should be so. I have been fortunate. We are a reading family. My mother and grandfather taught us to fill our minds with what would extend, not limit them.

Elinor And what did you fill yours with?

Jane Good heavens, child, there is all Shakespeare, and Milton, and Dr Johnson. There are the novels of Mr Fielding and Mr Richardson and Fanny Burney. There are . . .

Elinor (*severely*) But the novels of Mr Fielding are not genteel.

Elizabeth Mamma says that novels are not genteel at all . . .

Jane Gentility is a very limiting virtue. It is in the name of gentility that Elizabeth will marry a man she does not love—and Elinor . . . (*She pauses*)

Elinor You see—you can think of nothing to say about *my* future. (*Rising*) Oh, I am so afraid . . .

Jane (*moving quickly to Elinor*) Afraid, Elinor?

Elinor (*struggling with her tears*) I have no money, I am plain, I feel ridiculous. Who will ever look at me? I shall be an old maid, frightened, and poor and miserable . . .

Jane (*sitting on the sofa and drawing Elinor to sit beside her*) *I* am an old maid, Elinor.

Elinor Oh! I am sorry! I did not think . . .

Jane (*laughing*) But I like it. Is it a worse fate than being married to a sot, a bully or a fool? I am neither frightened nor unhappy.

Elinor Tell me how to be a happy old maid.

Jane Keep busy, with something worthwhile. (*Patting Elinor's hand*) Though I do not think you will be an old maid, Elinor. Remember, whether you are married or single, that it is sheer idleness that turns women into fools. They tittle-tattle about their shrubberies and ha-ha's, their caps and muslins, their servants and their menfolk, their routs and assemblies—oh, my dears, it is a thousand times better to be a servant, or a milliner, or have a little general shop like Miss Tranter . . .

Elizabeth But they have to *work* for their living. They . . .

Jane And they do useful work. (*Surveying them*) What can you do that is useful? Elinor?

Elinor (*diffidently*) I do not do anything really well . . .

Elizabeth (*rising and moving to the sofa*) Indeed you do. You draw quite nicely—oh yes, you do. She drew a portrait of me the other day and Mr Samson praised it. He said she had caught a likeness.

Jane And who is Mr Samson?

Elizabeth The rich gentleman I do not wish to marry. (*Mischievously, sitting on the sofa*) But Elinor does.

Jane (*looking at Elinor*) Does she, indeed?

Elinor (*hastily*) Elizabeth can play the pianoforte very prettily—far better than I can.

Jane Just so. And you can both embroider a little, paint a little, read the *Gentlewoman's Magazine*, cut out patterns for dresses you will never make, you are genteel and pretty . . .

Elinor (*dolefully*) Elizabeth is pretty.

Jane Well, well. We will come to that later, Elinor. In the meantime, tell me what is the *use* of all these ladylike accomplishments? Could you earn a living by them?

Elizabeth Earn? You mean work for money? Mamma would never allow it.

Elinor What is left for us but ladylike accomplishments?

Jane So marriage is the only possible career. At all costs a partner must be found, rich if possible, or at least respectable. In twenty years' time you will dwindle into a Mrs Nullis or a Mrs Browning and be showing some other local old autocrat round your shrubberies and improvements.

Elizabeth (*springing up*) Oh no! We must break free, we must, we must!

Jane Then do not accept what silly women tell you is a woman's role in life. *Question* everything. You feel that you have intelligence? Then do not stifle it. Put it to good use, as the women who work for their livings have to do.

Elinor You are not like Mrs Nullis and Mrs Browning and . . .

Elizabeth And Mamma. Say it, Elinor. It is true.

Elinor You said it was because you were busy. What do you do?

Jane We cannot afford to keep more than one servant, and that is no bad thing. My sister and I keep house for our widowed mother, and our brothers and their families visit us frequently. We are busy enough.

Elizabeth But you talked of using our brains. Housekeeping does not require so much intelligence, does it?

Jane If you have to cut your garment according to your cloth, it does. And then I scribble a little besides.

Elinor Scribble?

Elizabeth You mean you write? You write novels?

Jane I have done.

Elinor (*eagerly*) Like Mrs Radcliffe's? (*Confidentially*) We read *The Mysteries of Udolpho* in bed, in secret.

Elizabeth I'm sure my hair stood on end the whole time. It was so romantic and terrifying. Are your novels like that?

Jane (*laughing*) No, indeed. My writing is like painting a miniature. I work with so fine a brush that I produce little effect after much labour.

Elizabeth Are your stories published?

Jane I have published some.

Elinor (*puzzled*) But where do you find subjects? How do you invent thrilling adventures?

Jane I do not need to invent. Two or three families in a village provide all the material I want.

Elinor (*disappointedly*) A village? What is thrilling about a village? Your books must be full of people just like us.

Jane Well, never mind. I am concerned with you, not myself. What is this about a penniless lieutenant? Or do you not wish to talk about him?

Elizabeth I wish to talk about nothing else. (*Kneeling beside Jane*) It is Frank Newbold. I shall never love anyone so well as Frank, and his feelings are the same for me. But Mamma . . .

Jane Is looking for a better investment. Has your Frank any influential friends who might help him up the ladder?

Elizabeth No. He must depend entirely on his merits. And he has so many merits. Yet he'll be passed over for those who have influence behind them. (*She rises, distraught*) And this is the last day of his shore leave. He must be aboard ship in Portsmouth tomorrow night and Mamma knows it. So she has forbidden me to go out because she knows he must leave here by noon. (*In a crescendo of misery*) And I do not know where he sails for, nor for how long, nor what may happen to me while he is gone, nor whether he will be true if I cannot tell him that I will wait and wait and wait for him . . .

Jane (*rising*) But my brother's ship sails from Portsmouth tomorrow. Can Frank's ship be the *Elephant*?

Elizabeth Yes, it is, it is! Does your brother know Frank?

Jane (*after a second's pause*) Why, now I think of it I believe he did mention a young officer from this village, and that he promised well. So you see he *has* been noticed, and I will see to it that he continues to be observed.

Elizabeth Is—is your brother more than a lieutenant?

Jane (*kindly*) Yes. He is the commander—but then he has been in the Navy a great deal longer than Frank. I'm told he may well be an admiral before he is done. And so may Frank!

Elizabeth (*hugging Jane*) Oh, you are so good, so understanding.

Elinor I think you must have been in love yourself at one time.

Elizabeth Have you?

Jane Why, yes. I have.

Elizabeth What happened?

Jane (*quietly*) He died. Before we could marry—he died.

Elizabeth (*bursting into tears*) Oh, how terrible! What agony you must have endured. If anything happened to Frank, I should die, too. (*She sits below the french window*)

Jane Dying is not so easy. One has to go on living. That is sometimes harder.

Elinor And you never wanted to marry anyone else?

Jane I never found anyone to match him, you see. It's like trying to mend something that was once perfect. (*She moves to the window and stands looking out*) But if you cannot match the material, put it away in lavender and love it for what it was. (*After looking out for a moment, in a different tone*) By the way, Elizabeth, I can see something which might be of interest to you—in the lane at the bottom of the garden.

Elizabeth (*wiping her eyes, her back to the window*) What is it?

Jane It looked somewhat like the top of a naval officer's hat . . .

Elizabeth (*whirling round*) Frank! It must be! (*Running to the window*) It is! (*She turns, frantic*) Oh, what shall I do? What shall I do? Mamma forbade me to go out.

Jane Which way is the shrubbery?

Elizabeth What do I care about a shrubbery when my Frank is in the road?

Elinor (*pointing off*) It is over there.

Jane Good. This lane at the bottom of the garden. It is the one where Miss Tranter keeps her little shop, is it not?

Elinor Yes.

Jane Then, Miss Elizabeth, can you possibly help me? I grow so forgetful nowadays, and I have omitted to buy some button twist for my sister. It is really most urgent. Would you slip across to Miss Tranter's and get me some? (*She searches for coins in her bag*) Snuff colour will do.

Elizabeth But Mamma . . .

Jane Mamma will quite understand when I explain.

Elizabeth You mean . . . ?

Jane (*impatiently*) I mean will you run into the lane where Miss
Tranter keeps her shop and see—well, what you can see.

Elizabeth (*eagerly*) I'll fetch my bonnet.

Jane Bother your bonnet! (*Clapping her hands*) Out of the window, child. There's no time to waste.

Elizabeth opens the long window and vanishes

Elinor runs to the window and watches

Elinor Oh, I hope—I do so hope . . . Ah! (*A smile breaks over her
face*)

Jane What is it? (*She moves away, smiling to herself*)

Elinor The naval hat. It's disappeared. As if he's bent down and
—ah, now it's up again and walking along the lane.

Jane The hat is?

Elinor With him underneath it, of course. (*Pause*) Oh dear! The
hat is going the wrong way—not in Miss Tranter's direction at
all. (*Appalled*) She's forgotten the button twist!

Jane (*sitting*) I do not care a button for Miss Tranter or her
twist. Come here, Elinor.

Elinor stands beside her

Are your eyes very weak?

Elinor I did not know they were weak at all until my aunt told
me. I'm sure I see just as well without my spectacles.

Jane Give them to me. (*She looks through the spectacles*) I am
rather short-sighted, but these—(*trying them off and on*)—these
make no difference either way. It seems they are of clear
glass.

Elinor Why should my aunt . . . ?

Jane Ah, why indeed? (*She rises and goes to Elinor*) And why
does she make you scrape your hair back thus? And knot a
shawl so tightly over your pretty dress?

Elinor She says my chest is weak.

Jane (*loosening Elinor's hair*) And I suppose you did not know
that either, until your aunt told you?

Elinor (*innocently*) No, indeed. I was very sorry to hear it. I do
not want my aunt to be worried by my ill health.

Jane My poor sweet Elinor, she is much more likely to be worried by your robustness. Help me to loosen your shawl. (*She slips off Elinor's shawl and stands back to survey her*) Now, do not stand so crushed together, child, with your elbows tucked into your ribs and your hands clutched tightly in front of you as if you were perished with cold. Drop your hands. Now— lift your arms sideways—loosely, loosely. So. (*She drapes the shawl over Elinor's arms so that it hangs gracefully behind her*) Now. Smile at me.

Elinor tries, but shies diffidently away

Look in the mirror, then, and smile at what you see.

Elinor turns, looks in the mirror over the fireplace, and gives a gasp of pleasure; then smiles shyly at herself, before turning to smile at Jane

Now you are yourself. This is what the world should see, not what your aunt would have you become.

Elinor But why should she . . . ?

Jane (*brusquely*) Really, Elinor, it is time you grew up. Your aunt has one pretty daughter whom she wishes to make a good marriage. She does not want a pretty niece who might compete.

Elinor I cannot believe my aunt could be so calculating.

Jane Your aunt is also Elizabeth's mother. That could make her very calculating indeed.

Elinor (*bursting out*) But it is all for nothing! Elizabeth does not even *like* Mr Samson.

Jane And you do?

Elinor (*confused*) I did not say . . .

Jane You did not need to. So there you sat, like patience on a monument——

Elinor On a what?

Jane —staring at him through spectacles that you do not need, your hair stretched to its utmost limits, and tied up like a parcel.

Elinor (*timidly*) I think he quite likes me—but—well, he's been told I am clever, you see. So he always talks dreadfully seriously. He told me he enjoyed good conversation—and I could think of nothing to say. Because of course I am not clever at all— not as clever as Elizabeth. She has everything.

Jane So have you, you little goose. Dear me, your aunt has done her work well. Next time you see Mr Samson, look at him with those big eyes and listen to his good conversation. Do not trouble to reply to it. When men say they enjoy good conversation, they mean they enjoy having a good listener.

Elinor (*nervously*) I heard the garden door. They are coming back. (*She goes quickly to the window*)

Jane (*urgently*) Elinor, promise me never to bundle yourself in that shawl again, never to wear those spectacles and never to strain your hair back so that you look like a startled horse.

Elinor She will never let me. What will she say when she sees . . .

Jane Be what you *are*, and surprise your aunt. Stand up for yourself. Do not accept her estimate of you; accept mine instead.

Elinor What is that?

Jane That you are every whit as intelligent and pretty as your cousin. Whether you marry or not, make the best of yourself. Sssh!

Elinor looks out of the window. Jane sits demurely where she was first seated

Lady Charlotte, Mrs Hartley, Mrs Browning and Mrs Nullis enter, the two latter in the background and suitably mortified

Lady Charlotte sits on the sofa facing the window, and Mrs Hartley on a chair with her back to it, so that she does not at first see Elinor

Lady Charlotte (*as she moves to the sofa*) A wilderness, my dear Mrs Hartley, must be a *contrived* one, not a natural one. It is of no use in the world to leave things to nature. Nature never knows where to stop. So, a wilderness must be planned and planted with as much care as a formal garden. (*She sits*) As for your shrubbery, the paths will always be damp and slippery because the bushes press in upon them too closely. It is a thousand pities that my advice was not sought sooner.

Mars Hartley (*sitting*) I will see what can be done to improve it, Lady Charlotte, in accordance with your suggestions. It is most kind, most gracious . . .

Elinor, finding Mrs Hartley's back towards her, turns round. Mrs

Nullis, on her way to a chair, leans fawningly over the back of the sofa

Mrs Nullis I am sure you remember me, Lady Charlotte. We met in Bath, at the Assembly Rooms. Mrs Robinson introduced——

Lady Charlotte (*cutting in, sharply, looking through her lorgnettes*) Who is that young woman? She was not here before.

Mrs Hartley Which young woman? (*She turns, sees Elinor, and springs to her feet*) Elinor! What are you thinking of, child? Where are your spectacles? And your shawl? You know that you must take care of that delicate chest.

Elinor (*after a frightened glance at Jane*) My—my chest is not delicate, Aunt. No doctor has ever told me so, and I have fewer colds than Elizabeth.

Mrs Hartley Upon my word, miss!

Elinor As for my spectacles, I find they are of clear glass. And I shall not wear them again unless a qualified medical man says they are necessary.

Mrs Hartley Ungrateful girl! All the care I have lavished on you, all the measures for your health, set at naught. Lady Charlotte, you see how I am defied by one whom I have taken into my own house, regarded as my own daughter . . .

Lady Charlotte Have you indeed?

Mrs Hartley Indeed I have.

Lady Charlotte I would not have thought so. I go out to look at your unfortunate shrubbery, leaving behind me one pretty daughter and one excessively plain niece, to whose plainness you took some pains to draw my attention. I return to find one pretty girl, but she is not your daughter, but that same niece. Are you entertaining me to a charade, Mrs Hartley?

Mrs Hartley (*beside herself*) No, but I think she is. Come here, girl.

Elinor goes to Mrs Hartley

What do you mean by loosening your hair in this fashion, you minx? An intellectual young lady with brains such as yours does not go about in ringlets.

Lady Charlotte (*in a voice of deep horror*) *Brains?* Did I hear you mention *brains* in connection with this unfortunate young woman?

Mrs Hartley I did. She is the clever one of the family.

Lady Charlotte My dear young lady. If you have pretensions to brains you should certainly conceal them. A girl should always try to make the best of herself. Brains are *not* a ladylike attribute.

Jane You remember, Elinor, that I told you such would be Lady Charlotte's opinion.

Lady Charlotte (*to Jane*) I am glad you understand me so well, ma'am.

Mrs Hartley But Lady Charlotte . . .!

Lady Charlotte Come closer, girl.

Elinor stands before Lady Charlotte and is surveyed

You appear to have made a vast improvement in yourself during our short absence. Who knows what a little more time might achieve? The chin—(*she tips Elinor's chin with her lorgnettes*)—should be carried higher. The shoulders—(*she taps Elinor's shoulders*)—less droopingly, the bosom more pronounced. That is well, very well, miss. You have almost the confidence of your cousin.

Mrs Hartley (*reminded of her daughter*) Elizabeth! Where is Elizabeth? Elinor, where has she gone? I expressly . . .

Elizabeth bounds in through the window, her face radiant

Elizabeth Oh, Elinor, Elinor—— (*She stops, appalled, facing her mother*)

Mrs Hartley Ay, you, miss. Where have you been? Did I not tell you——

Lady Charlotte (*interrupting*) Mrs Hartley! I was speaking and giving my attention to your niece. I am not accustomed to being interrupted by family brawls.

Mrs Hartley Forgive me, Lady Charlotte. I am so distraught that I scarcely know what I am doing. (*She moves back, palpitating*)

Lady Charlotte To be distraught because your daughter has ventured into the garden at eleven in the morning seems to indicate an excessively nervous disposition.

Jane (*rising*) I am the culprit, Mrs Hartley. I asked Elizabeth to fetch me some thread from Miss Tranter's.

A gasp from Elizabeth shows that she has forgotten the commission. She looks at the coin in her hand. Jane smoothly goes to her and takes back the coin as she speaks

And I fear your trouble was for nothing, dear Elizabeth, for I can see that Miss Tranter *still* has not procured the colour I wanted. It is most provoking, but thank you, my dear, for trying.

Lady Charlotte Am I to understand, Miss Elizabeth, that you went beyond the garden and into the street, without your bonnet?

Elizabeth nods, speechless

That, Mrs Hartley, is a grave social error indeed. I understand your concern.

Elizabeth (*with a quick glance at Jane, but curtseying meekly*) I am sorry, Lady Charlotte. I will remember your words. They show clearly the standards by which you judge a woman's worth.

Lady Charlotte (*majestically*) Then let them be remembered.

Jane (*going to Mrs Hartley*) You will forgive me, Mrs Hartley, if I take my leave a little early? I must be home in time to help with the dinner. Good day, Lady Charlotte. Mrs Nullis. Mrs Browning.

They bow to each other

Pray, madam, do not trouble to come to the door. I am sure Elizabeth and Elinor will do that.

Jane, Elizabeth and Elinor go out

Lady Charlotte (*incredulously*) To help with the dinner? Gracious heavens, Mrs Hartley, who was that person? And when did she come in?

Mrs Hartley (*sitting*) She has been here all the time, Lady Charlotte.

Mrs Nullis (*with asperity*) And was as little noticed as the rest of us, it seems.

Lady Charlotte Persons who are not noticed are generally beneath it. As, I imagine, is anyone who has to "help with the dinner".

Mrs Browning Her father was a clergyman, long since deceased.
And she lives in the village with her mother and sister.
Lady Charlotte And cooks the dinner!

Elizabeth and Elinor enter, Elizabeth admiring Elinor's changed appearance

Mrs Hartley Oh, she is not a person of any consequence, Lady
Charlotte.
Mrs Nullis Of no consequence in the world.
Mrs Browning She appears to have no conversation except for
button twist and cooking and the like.
Elinor (*protesting*) But she is very clever. Isn't she, Elizabeth?
Elizabeth Of course she is. She writes books.
Lady Charlotte *Books?* What sort of books?
Elizabeth Novels. (*She sits*)
Elinor And some of them are published.
Lady Charlotte *Novels?* I trust, Mrs Hartley, that you do not
allow your young people to read anything as immoral as a
novel?
Mrs Hartley Indeed, Lady Charlotte, except for the Bible and
Fordyce's sermons, I do not allow them access to the printed
word at all.
Lady Charlotte Even the Bible, Mrs Hartley, needs expurgating
by that excellent Mr Bowdler who is doing so much to render
Shakespeare fit for refined ears. But novels . . . !
Elizabeth (*with spirit*) She writes nothing immoral or in bad taste,
I am sure. She lives quietly in the village.
Lady Charlotte In that case, child, she can know nothing of the
world, and consequently can have nothing to write about.
Mrs Nullis True, Lady Charlotte. Why, what material could she
draw on? She does not move in high society, she does not
travel, she has no more education than the rest of us.
Mrs Browning What novels could possibly emerge from our
select circle?
Lady Charlotte If you allow writers of crude fiction into it, Mrs
Hartley, your circle is less select than you imagine. Kindly call
my carriage.

Mrs Hartley pulls a bell-rope

Mrs Hartley Oh, Lady Charlotte, I hope you will take no offence over this matter. Her father *was* a clergyman.

Lady Charlotte I am not impressed by the clergy. They are slightly above the lower orders and far below the upper ones. One hardly knows where to place them. (*She rises*) Their smattering of education gives them ideas above their station which their stipends do not allow them to support. So much for the clergy.

The Maid enters

Mrs Hartley Lady Charlotte's carriage, please.

The Maid bobs and goes

Lady Charlotte (*moving to the door then turning*) That person. What is her name?

Mrs Hartley Austen, Lady Charlotte.

Mrs Nullis Miss Jane Austen.

Lady Charlotte I am glad to say I have never heard of her. Miss Austen is, as you say, a person of no consequence. (*She turns to go*)

Elizabeth (*springing to her feet*) A person of no consequence? You are wrong, Lady Charlotte.

Lady Charlotte (*revolving, disbelief on her countenance*) Wrong? I am never wrong!

Elinor Miss Austen is a person of the very greatest consequence.

Mrs Hartley Elizabeth! Elinor!

Lady Charlotte How dare such chits of girls . . .

Elizabeth I am a chit who is regarded as old enough to marry. And if we are old enough for that we are old enough to defend our friends against ignorance and prejudice.

Elinor You see I have taken your advice, Lady Charlotte. I am holding my chin high.

Mrs Hartley Lady Charlotte, this is some madness—I shall punish them severely.

Lady Charlotte Do not distress yourself, Mrs Hartley. I shall not be visiting your establishment again. It was a mistake ever to do so. As for your young people—words fail me!

Lady Charlotte sweeps out

Elizabeth If only they would!
Mrs Hartley Oh! Oh! Oh!

Tableau: The two girls laughing together, Mrs Browning and Mrs Nullis gazing at them in horror, Mrs Hartley collapsed in hysterics on the sofa. The music holds it, as—

the CURTAIN *falls*

FURNITURE AND PROPERTY LIST

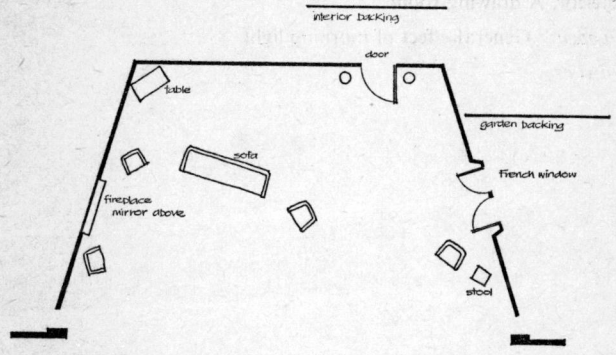

On stage: Sofa
    4 chairs
    Stool
    Occasional table. *On it:* tray with madeira wine and glasses,
        cake on plate, knife, 4 small plates
    Other occasional tables, etc. as dressing

Over mantelpiece: mirror
    Beside mantelpiece: bell-rope
    Carpet
    Window curtains

Personal: **Elinor:** spectacles
    Lady Charlotte: lorgnettes
    Jane: bag with coins

LIGHTING PLOT

Property fittings required: nil
Interior. A drawing-room

To open: General effect of morning light

No cues

EFFECTS PLOT

Cue 1   As CURTAIN rises   (Page 1)
           Music: continue until action starts

Cue 2   **Mrs Hartley:** "Oh! Oh! Oh!"   (Page 20)
           Music: continue until Curtain falls